Potty Project:

Let's Learn Together!

Nicole Minard

Illustrations by Blueberry Illustrations

ISBN: 9798878939591

THE STORY BEGINS......

Projects are fun.
Projects are great.
When projects are done,
we get to celebrate!

Crayons and paint
are messy and cool.
We can also use projects
to learn how to Pee Pee and Poo.

First: gather your materials.
Next: have a plan.
After you potty, make sure
to wash your hands!

Practice and practice, try, try again.
Soon you'll go on the potty...
I know that you can!

While you are playing, check if you're dry.
You did it! You're clean! Can I have a high five?

Need to go potty? Give it a try!
We can walk, we can run,
or take the train by.

(Chugga chugga choo choo,
the potty is where we go
Pee Pee and Poo Poo)

There's no need to rush.
Get cozy while you sit.
Waiting, still waiting...
It could take a bit.
If nothing comes out, take another sip!

Sitting and waiting, time is slow as can be,
But I am a potty champ, just wait and you'll see!

Back to playing, stay dry, then another sit.
Wait... do you hear that sound?

You peed in the potty, you did it, you did it!!!

Keep practicing and remember...
What goes on the potty?
Pee pee and poo!
Your Potty Project is going great,
and I am so proud of you!

THE END

Nicole Minard is both a mother and a Behavior Analyst who knows that parenting is an incredible journey and tries to appreciate all the little, wonderful moments. Nicole is passionate about empowering parents with valuable tools for navigating the parenting journey. She believes if you can be confident in your parenting, you can replace stress with joy.

With a wealth of experience in Applied Behavior Analysis and a deep understanding of child development, she has crafted "Potty Project: Let's Learn Together!" to infuse fun and creativity into these important milestones.

Nicole believes that every family deserves a positive and supportive learning experience, and this book embodies that commitment. When not writing, she enjoys spending time with her own family, cherishing the small, everyday moments of parenting and the joys of watching children grow. Driven by her passion, Nicole has embarked on various ventures, including founding an ABA agency, nurturing a babysitting organization, and creating the 'Living Full Well' collection. This collection is her way of helping parents like you feel confident and fulfilled in your parenting journey.

Join Nicole on this delightful adventure to make potty training memorable and enjoyable for both children and caregivers. You can connect with Nicole on Instagram or explore her website at LivingFullWell.com to share your own potty training stories and experiences. Parenthood is a journey worth celebrating!

www.ingramcontent.com/pod-product-compliance
Lightning Source LLC
Chambersburg PA
CBHW042130110726
48006CB00003B/826

* 9 7 9 8 3 3 0 4 5 5 3 6 2 *